LEARNING TO LEAD

An Action Plan for Success

Pat Heim, Ph.D.
Elwood N. Chapman

CRISP PUBLICATIONS, INC.
Los Altos, California

LEARNING TO LEAD
An Action Plan for Success

Pat Heim, Ph.D.
Elwood N. Chapman

CREDITS
Editor: **Michael Crisp**
Designer: **Carol Harris**
Layout and Composition: **Interface Studio**
Cover Design: **Carol Harris**
Artwork: **Ralph Mapson**

Copyright © 1990 by Crisp Publications, Inc.
Printed in the United States of America

Crisp books are distributed in Canada by Reid Publishing, Ltd., P.O. Box 7267, Oakville, Ontario, Canada L6J 6L6.

In Australia by Career Builders, P.O. Box 1051, Springwood, Brisbane, Queensland, Australia 4127.

And in New Zealand by Career Builders, P.O. Box 571, Manurewa, New Zealand.

Library of Congress Catalog Card Number 90-80571
Heim, Pat and Chapman, Elwood N.
Learning to Lead
ISBN 1-56052-043-4

TO THE READER

Which would you prefer to be called? An excellent manager or an excellent leader? Maybe you haven't considered the differences between the two, but most people would rather be designated as an excellent leader because it suggests a quality that goes beyond basic management skills.

The purpose of this book is to enhance your present management abilities with a stronger, more discernible dimension. In short, this book was developed to help sharpen your leadership skills. It assumes you are already familiar with what it takes to become a good manager. As most leaders recognize, becoming a capable manager is a requirement before one will be regarded as a good leader.

Solid management skills provide the foundation upon which to build a leadership dimension. These skills remain essential during the leadership building process. Also, after becoming a leader, you must *maintain* your management competencies. It is the combination of both management and leadership skills that will provide the formula for your success.

Do most managers possess the basic ability to become leaders? Yes, but only if their desire is sufficiently intense. Such a challenge requires behavioral changes. These can only be made with hard work and repetition. It is therefore suggested that you read this book in its entirety before deciding the level of commitment you are willing to accept.

If you decide to initiate a Leader/Manager improvement program, you will want to follow the advice presented on a page-by-page basis. Taken seriously, the contents of this book constitute a powerful program that produces positive results.

The decision is yours. Good luck!

Elwood N. Chapman

Pat Heim

i

ABOUT THIS BOOK

LEARNING TO LEAD is not like most books. It has a unique self-paced format that encourages a reader to become personally involved. Designed to be "read with a pencil," there is an abundance of exercises, activities, assessments and cases that invite participation.

The objective of LEARNING TO LEAD is to provide the fundamentals of both good management *and* leadership skills.

LEARNING TO LEAD (and the other self-improvement titles listed on the order form in the back of this book) can be used effectively in a number of ways. Here are some possibilities:

—Individual Study. Because the book is self-instructional, all that is needed is a quiet place, some time and a pencil. By completing the activities and exercises, a reader will not only receive valuable feedback, but also practical steps for self-improvement.

—Workshops and Seminars. This book is ideal for assigned reading prior to a workshop or seminar. With the basics in hand, the quality of the participation will improve and more time can be spent on concept extentions and applications during the program. The book is also effective when it is distributed at the beginning of a session, and participants "work through" the contents.

—Remote Location Training. Books can be sent to those not able to attend "home office" training sessions.

There are many other possibilities that depend on the objectives, program or ideas of the user.

One thing for sure. Even after this book has been read, it will be looked at—and thought about—again and again.

CONTENTS

CONTENTS (Continued)

P A R T

I

What Is Your Leadership Potential?

FIRST: TAKE THE LEADERSHIP POTENTIAL ASSESSMENT

LEADERSHIP POTENTIAL SCALE

If you expect to become a manager or already occupy a management position, you may wonder whether or not you have the potential to lead others. This exercise is designed to help you reach this decision. Read the statement at both ends of the scale and then circle the number that best indicates where you belong. Most people fall somewhere between the two extremes.

	HIGH									LOW	
I can be both an excellent manager and have time to lead.	10	9	8	7	6	5	4	3	2	1	I am satisfied being a good manager.
I am a visionary. I love to plan for long-term goals.	10	9	8	7	6	5	4	3	2	1	Getting by one day at a time is my goal.
Risk-taking is my cup of tea. It challenges me.	10	9	8	7	6	5	4	3	2	1	I avoid risks whenever possible.
It is a challenge to discipline others.	10	9	8	7	6	5	4	3	2	1	I do not enjoy having to discipline others.
I enjoy communication and have the potential to become outstanding.	10	9	8	7	6	5	4	3	2	1	My communication skills are adequate.
I have the desire to become a top leader.	10	9	8	7	6	5	4	3	2	1	I'm comfortable as a follower.
I enjoy making tough decisions.	10	9	8	7	6	5	4	3	2	1	Decisions can be frustrating and scary.
I seek and welcome more responsibility	10	9	8	7	6	5	4	3	2	1	I avoid added responsibilities.
I can handle the pressure of being in the limelight under fire.	10	9	8	7	6	5	4	3	2	1	Pressure is not for me.
I believe I have the personality to become a successful leader.	10	9	8	7	6	5	4	3	2	1	Sorry, I'm not the leadership type.

TOTAL ☐

If you scored 80 or above, it would appear that you have a high desire and potential to be a leader. A rating between 60 and 80 shows good potential. A rating under 60 is a signal you may wish to delay weaving leadership practices into your management style.

DIFFERENCES BETWEEN MANAGERS AND LEADER/MANAGERS

Explaining the differences between managers and leaders can be difficult to define. Recognizing this, the following statements may help you distinguish your dimensions of leadership. Please place a ✔ in the appropriate box depending on whether you agree or disagree with the following statements:

AGREE   **DISAGREE**

☐   ☐   A good manager is content to simply follow directions and suggestions from above. A Leader/Manager is more apt to consider the future, and anticipate needs, problems and issues before being told that action is needed.

☐   ☐   A good manager is willing to accept responsibility. A Leader/Manager seeks responsibility.

☐   ☐   An effective manager will take modest risks (when the odds are favorable). A Leader/Manager accepts higher risks when they have the potential to result in greater progress, and commits to a plan of action with greater determination.

☐   ☐   A Leader/Manager has more of an ''entrepreneurial spirit'' than a basic manager.

☐   ☐   A manager is more apt to accept comfortable assignments while a leader looks for more demanding opportunities to demonstrate his or her leadership potential.

☐   ☐   A manager usually views those under his or her supervision as employees. A leader views employees as team members and followers.

☐   ☐   A basic difference between managers and leaders is attitude. Many managers are content to set modest goals, pacify others, try for a comfortable working environment and use power cautiously. A leader tends to set more demanding goals, challenges others, and creates a more dynamic working environment.

If you checked Agree on all boxes, you should find that the ideas presented in this book will be comfortable to practice and incorporate in your daily activities.

ARE ONLY SOLID MANAGERS FREE TO LEAD?

Leadership at any level is built on basic management skills. Until an operation is well managed, the person in charge is not sufficiently free to lead. Thus those attempting to lead without fundamental management competencies usually fail before they get started.

> "You can't lead an organization if you are constantly putting out management-related fires."
>
> "Some weeks it is all I can do to act as a caretaker around here. Lead? You've got to be kidding."
>
> "I feel apologetic about the fact that I can free myself to lead only now and then."

A few individuals are in a high enough position to select and train good administrative personnel who can free them to lead. But a first level manager who desires to lead must learn to manage efficiently in such a way that she or he has the freedom to add the leadership dimension to their style. This means that managers who want to lead must free themselves by learning to be:

- superior teachers, counselors, and delegators.

- outstanding time managers who are good at setting priorities and establishing goals.

- excellent system and control developers and operators.

What are the dangers of reaching into leadership behaviors before excellent management practices are in position?

It is possible to wind up in limbo and lose your management job.

Confusing leadership with management skills can leave you (the would-be leader) frustrated.

Employees can feel insecure or lose respect for the way you operate.

First things first. Hone your management skills before jumping into leadership situations.

NOTES

PART

II

Is Leadership For You?

MAKING A LEADERSHIP COMMITMENT

Not everyone aspires to lead. Some capable, valuable individuals are content to be excellent managers. These people prefer the recognition that comes from good management techniques. They leave visionary risks to others. At a certain point in their careers they would rather "follow" as a manager than lead others from a more demanding position. Their management position gives them all the leadership responsibility they desire or need.

What about you?

Listed below are three major reasons why most managers elect to improve their leadership potential. Read each statement and place a ☑ in the square that most accurately reflects your feelings.

	Exactly how I feel.	Somewhat the way I feel.	Not the way I feel.
1. I seek more personal fulfillment than I can achieve in a management role. I want to feel I have improved the destiny of my organization. I am fearful I will get lost in the crowd if I don't step out of a pure management position.	☐	☐	☐
2. As a manager, I feel "boxed in." I want freedom to make more decisions and more power to execute them. Taking more risks will keep me motivated and I will come closer to reaching my full potential as a person.	☐	☐	☐
3. I want upward mobility. I want to climb the executive ladder higher and faster. Money is important, but even more important is my desire to achieve some really meaningful long-term goals.	☐	☐	☐

INVITATION TO A THREE-STEP
CHALLENGE

STEP 1: Carefully complete the Management Assessment Scale on the page that follows.

STEP 2: While reading this book, try to keep the differences between a successful manager and a leader clear in your mind.

STEP 3: Complete the Management/Leadership Assessment Scale on page 65 and compare with your score on page 11.

MANAGEMENT ASSESSMENT SCALE

This survey describes twenty (20) practices that are common to excellent managers. Please read all statements carefully. Then decide as a present or future manager the priority you would assign each practice or characteristic. Indicate your decision by circling the appropriate number.

	PRIORITY				
	Highest	High	Important	Modest	Low
1. Strives to keep employees fully informed.	5	4	3	2	1
2. Expresses thoughts clearly.	5	4	3	2	1
3. Good listener.	5	4	3	2	1
4. Shows compassion.	5	4	3	2	1
5. Provides important rewards to staff.	5	4	3	2	1
6. Wins by allowing employees to also win.	5	4	3	2	1
7. Has full backing from those under him/her.	5	4	3	2	1
8. Provides structure to create cohesive feeling.	5	4	3	2	1
9. Establishes consistent, clear discipline lines.	5	4	3	2	1
10. Gets tough when needed.	5	4	3	2	1
11. Respected by employees when authority is used.	5	4	3	2	1
12. Uses power with sensitivity.	5	4	3	2	1
13. Consults with others in making decisions.	5	4	3	2	1
14. Follows logical steps in making decisions.	5	4	3	2	1
15. Admits to mistakes.	5	4	3	2	1
16. Maintains positive, upbeat attitude.	5	4	3	2	1
17. Makes work enjoyable.	5	4	3	2	1
18. Shares large and small victories with staff.	5	4	3	2	1
19. Delegates effectively.	5	4	3	2	1
20. Highly ethical in all situations.	5	4	3	2	1

TOTAL SCORE ☐

Later in this book you will be invited to prioritize the above management characteristics *along with twenty (20) leadership practices*. This unique process will help you differentiate between management and leadership skills. It will also provide insight into the future role you desire for yourself.

NOTES

P A R T

III

Developing Your
Leadership
Power Sources

EVERYONE HAS UNUSED PERSONALITY POWER

Personality power is the development and use of your best traits to influence others. It is being the best you can be—*on a personal basis.* When you hear someone say "my manager motivates us" you are hearing a message about the power of a positive personality. Everyone has a unique personality that can be transmitted effectively to others. Some individuals may be blessed with more power than others, but all of us possess more power than we realize. And it is not how much power we have, but rather how we use what we possess.

Personality power is expressed through both physical *and* mental traits. Personality power is transmitted when people make the most of their *best* traits. They have learned to isolate these special traits that impress others and concentrate on improving and transmitting them. In this way, they learn to increase their personality power.

Personality power is important to leaders. Without personality power followers would not be inspired to reach for new goals. Leaders must use their power to *influence.* They generate as much personality power as possible and use it wisely. The purpose of Part I is to help you develop your personality power.

PLAY UP YOUR BEST TRAITS

Not too long ago, psychologists and management experts believed it took a special combination of personality traits (distinguishing characteristics) to become a successful leader. No one, however, was able to prove what many people started to call the Trait Theory. Today, experts agree that there are so many acceptable traits—in so many combinations and mixes—that virtually anyone has a degree of personality power. In other words, you are not disqualified as a potential leader if you wear glasses, are unusually tall or you prefer to read books rather than work out in the health club.

To become a successful leader, however, you *do* need to identify and develop a mix of your best traits and then learn to communicate them effectively. This is the major challenge you face as you commit to put more leadership into your management style. Ask yourself these questions:

Can I recognize and communicate my best physical characteristics?

Is there room for improvement in my verbal skills?

Do I have some good mental traits that I should feature and communicate more frequently?

What role should attitude play in my personality power package?

The road to take if you wish to have more influence over others is to emphasize your special, distinguishable traits. Do not be over-concerned with personal traits you would prefer to be different—simply identify, improve, and transmit your best traits. For example, if you have attractive hair, highlight it. If you have more patience than others, use this trait to gain compliments. If you have a full, authoritative voice, use it to your advantage. In other words, *play your winners!*

THREE SOURCES OF LEADERSHIP POWER

1. PERSONALITY POWER

To understand the potential of your personality power, it is necessary to appreciate two other primary sources, role power and knowledge power. The illustration below gives personality power the biggest segment, but it would be a mistake to underestimate the possible power of the other two.

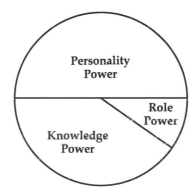

WHAT ARE OTHER POWER SOURCES?

2. ROLE POWER

Role power comes from the position you hold. This is not power that comes from knowledge or experience. It is not power that comes from your personality traits. Role power goes with your position regardless of who occupies it. The moment someone is promoted into the role of a supervisor, they gain power. We have all witnessed the abuse of role power, even at the lowest level.

3. KNOWLEDGE POWER

Knowledge power comes from understanding the skills and techniques required for effective behavior in a given role. As our society becomes increasingly technical and roles become more specialized, knowledge power becomes more and more important.

When someone decides to work to build their skills, power sources come quickly into play. When this happens, the following considerations surface:

- How can one make sensitive use of all power sources?

- When is it best to draw power from one source as opposed to another?

- How does one achieve the perfect or best "balance" in the daily utilization of all three sources?

These, and other questions, will be answered on the following pages.

DOWNPLAY YOUR ROLE POWER

As a manager you have been given some authority over others. Those above you may have more power, but this does not diminish what you have received. As a leader, however, you may improve your value to the organization by assuming you have slightly more role power. As a new manager you must still downplay your role power in comparison to that of your other two sources.

You are the designated "boss" so you lead the team. But keep in mind that without the role, your power may not yet be established. This means you will want to make the best possible use of role power but be humble enough to recognize that no matter whom occupies the role, *the power is still there.* Role power is a temporary franchise. With this in mind, please AGREE or DISAGREE with the following statements by checking the appropriate square.

AGREE   **DISAGREE**

☐   ☐   A true leader does not need to remind team members that he or she is in charge.

☐   ☐   The more effectively you use knowledge and personality power, the less you will need to use role power.

☐   ☐   The best use of role power is to maintain discipline. Sometimes it must be used to restore structure so that everyone can reach their productivity potential.

☐   ☐   It is possible to communicate your role power through your actions and activities.

☐   ☐   When people respect you as a person they are more likely to respect the role you occupy.

☐   ☐   When someone says "the new supervisor's job has gone to his or her head" the individual means that role power is being abused.

☐   ☐   It is not easy to live with newly acquired role power, especially at the beginning.

☐   ☐   Leaders who seek more role power must learn how to use it in a sensitive manner at the very beginning.

PLAY UP YOUR KNOWLEDGE POWER

Many managers and leaders foolishly downplay knowledge as a power source. Knowledge power may be the safest and best way to demonstrate leadership. Reflect for a moment on why most people respect mentors. Isn't it because the mentor provides knowledge and guidance? If you agree, then you should strive to be both a mentor and a leader to your staff. In other words, be an outstanding *teacher*. Share your knowledge. Take time to give insructions in a clear and complete manner. Turn your employees into followers by using knowledge to build a better relationship with them.

With the above in mind, please AGREE or DISAGREE with the following statement by checking the appropriate square.

AGREE   **DISAGREE**

☐   ☐   Leaders need to be more sensitive to and generous in sharing their knowledge.

☐   ☐   Of the three sources, knowledge power is the best way to earn respect from a staff member.

☐   ☐   The more you know about your job or business, the more knowledge power you have. Translated, this means the best use of knoweldge power is to continue to learn.

☐   ☐   It is possible to overuse knowledge power and wind up being viewed as a "know-it-all."

☐   ☐   Your personality power is the best way to communicate your knowledge power.

☐   ☐   One need not be as sensitive in the use of knowledge power as is true of role power.

☐   ☐   Most managers and leaders have more knowledge power than they realize, thus they tend to underuse it.

☐   ☐   Practical experience is an excellent way to gain more knowledge power.

CAPITALIZE ON YOUR DIFFERENT PHYSICAL TRAITS

When you ask someone to name a leader, you may be surprised. The leader may have an image far different from what you anticipated. This may be because leaders sometimes recognize the importance of featuring their distinguishing features. Sometimes these features may not fit into normal expectations. Some leaders are short (Napolean). Some have big noses (DeGaulle). Some disregard traditional grooming standards (Lincoln).

Most leaders, however, command attention. Think of the bearing displayed by tribal chieftains. Compare historical leaders such as Einstein, Churchill, or Sister Teresa. All make the most of a few physical traits that are unattractive in the traditional sense.

Ask yourself this question: ''If I strengthen one or more of my unusual features, will it communicate more personality power than if I try to improve some of my less noticeable traits?'' In most cases the answer is yes. Followers want their leaders to be different. They want their leaders to stand out. They do not ask their leaders to win beauty contests.

Listed below are ten physical characteristics. Identify the three that you feel distinguish you most from other people. To do this, simply circle the appropriate words. If you have a different trait (not listed), add it in the space provided.

EYES	HAIR/BEARD	POSTURE/FIGURE	SMILE
	FACIAL COUNTENANCE	BEARING SIZE GROOMING	
COMPLEXION	GENERAL IMAGE	OTHER _____	

If you are interested in communicating a more serious ''leadership image'' than in the past, consider highlighting the features you checked. Not only will people accept you more easily, but you will feel more comfortable with yourself. This, in turn, will give you more self-confidence.

MORE CONFIDENCE EQUALS MORE PERSONALITY POWER!

FEATURE YOUR BEST MENTAL TRAITS

It is more difficult to pinpoint strong mental characteristics than to recognize physical traits. Yet, as a leader, it is important to be known to have a few unusual traits that followers appreciate.

Listed below are some mental characteristics that help followers feel more secure. Please circle the three that you feel are the strongest in your personal inventory. Or, if you prefer, circle three that you respect the most and want to strengthen in the future.

PATIENCE   INTEGRITY   TACT   COURAGE   MEMORY

DISCIPLINE   DECISIVENESS   FAIRNESS   CONSISTENCY

ABILITY TO TAKE PRESSURE   BOUNCE-BACK ABILITY

WILLINGNESS TO ACCEPT RESPONSIBILITY   DETERMINATION

WILLINGNESS TO TAKE RISKS   POSITIVE ATTITUDE

OTHER _____

You have now selected three of your differential mental traits. Three that stand out as values, standards, in your behavioral patterns. Of course, *all* of the mental traits will help you become a better leader, but the idea is to be known to have a few that are outstanding. One way to accomplish this is to *play up* the three you selected without neglecting the others. In doing this, be true to yourself. For example, if you selected decisiveness, consistency, and willingness to accept responsibility, it would work to your advantage if people recognized these qualities in you and talked about them openly in making an evaluation of your leadership abilities.

PEOPLE FIND IT EASIER TO ACCEPT AN INDIVIDUAL AS THEIR LEADER WHEN THEY RECOGNIZE VALUED MENTAL TRAITS AND STANDARDS.

CULTIVATE A MORE AUTHORITATIVE VOICE

Some years back, the author of this book interviewed sixty recognized leaders and made a point of asking this question: ''What helped you most become a leader?'' Almost half replied that their ''public speaking'' ability provided the greatest assistance.

Have you taken time to listen to your voice recently? If not, why not tape your voice and play it back from either a recorder or telephone answering device. Is it dull or vibrant? Draggy or crisp? Strong or weak? Choice of words is important, but the *way* you say words (diction) is also significant. It may inspire you to know that Eleanor Roosevelt took elocution lessons as First Lady and wound up as our representative to the United Nations, where her voice was heard around the world.

It is possible to train your voice to be clear, strong and decisive. A strong voice will help you put more authority into your message and will communicate more leadership. This single trait is only one feature, but *it can make a difference.* If you are confident of your voice, you will be more confident speaking to groups and this confidence will translate into all of your communications.

Here are some simple suggestions to improve your speaking abilities:

- If you desire to improve your abilities as a speaker, consider taking a course or join a speaker's organization, such as Toastmasters.

- Believe in what you are saying.

- Avoid using ''non-words'' such as uhhh or ummm.

- Refrain from making excuses or qualifying what you say with ''if's'' and ''maybe's.''

- Except in cases where a tough situation is being faced and a line is being drawn, keep a smile on your face and communicate a positive attitude.

- Learn not to overtalk: Recognize it is not how much you say, but what the listener hears and accepts.

- Balance everything you say by also being a good listener.

- Order *The Art of Communicating* or *Effective Presentation Skills*, using the form in the back of this book.

TRAIN YOUR VOICE TO PUT MORE POWER INTO YOUR PERSONALITY.

DISCOVER YOUR OWN
BRAND OF CHARISMA

Charisma is a certain charm that is defined as a "psychological attraction." Charisma causes others to react to a person in a more positive way than would normally be the case. Sometimes, by emphasizing our "differential traits," we can create a "charisma" that was not previously discernible. More often charisma is the result of natural selection—that is, a few special traits blended together in our personality makeup.

Is personality the same as charisma? Not exactly. Personality consists of *all* physical and mental characteristics of an individual that transmitted as images to another person. Charisma occurs when a mix of a few attractive characters "blend together" to create a special charm.

Do all leaders have charisma? No. Most leaders, in fact, recognize they do not have charisma but, nevertheless, make the most of their personalities. In a short, informal survey many of those responding suggested that only about 10% of leaders had charisma. This does not mean that charisma is not desirable. It is. But most leaders know they can develop the personality power required to be effective without having charisma.

When successful managers decide to stress leadership, they are wise to play up their best physical and mental characteristics (be the best they can be with what they possess) and not be concerned with whether or not the changes they make will make them charismatic. As will be presented in the next stages of this book, leadership is much more than personality.

DON'T UNDERESTIMATE THE MAGIC OF YOUR POSITIVE ATTITUDE

Few would disagree that attitude is the most significant and powerful characteristic in anyone's personality inventory. A positive, vibrant attitude is often the ingredient that highlights all other favorable traits. A positive attitude is necessary to project a winning leadership image—charismatic or not. A positive attitude is recognized as the ''magic'' that transmits the best of anyone's personality. A negative attitude closes the door.

Attitude is simply the way you view the world around you. It is a perceptual or mental phenomena. It is your focus on life. In a sense, you see what you want to see. If you concentrate on negative factors (and there are plenty) you eventually will wind up with a negative attitude. When you concentrate on positive factors, you are more apt to stay positive. It sounds easy when you say ''look at the bright side,'' but, of course, it isn't. A positive attitude can be everyone's most priceless possession.[1] To a leader it is essential.

Attitude is also the way you look at yourself. If you see yourself as a successful manager, chances are that you will be one. If you also see yourself as a successful leader, it is more likely to occur. Consider these possibilities:

- When you are positive, all around you are positively influenced.

- A positive attitude converts a personality that is easy to ignore into one that isn't.

- A leader with a negative attitude doesn't keep followers for long.

- People reach their personality potential when they have a positive attitude.

- Individuals are more creative when they are positive.

- A positive attitude releases the enthusiasm stored up inside individuals—as a result, they have more confidence to play out their roles as leaders.

---

[1]Order *Attitude: Your Most Priceless Possession,* a Crisp publication similar to the one you are reading, using the form in the back of this book.

CASE STUDY 1:

SELECTING THE BEST AVAILABLE MODEL

Crystal devoted the first several months following her promotion to becoming an excellent manager. She read extensively and took all available seminars on management-related topics. She applied techniques and principles alike. Her superiors were more than pleased with her performance.

During this period, Crystal fashioned her behavior around a manager who turned out to be a mentor. Then it occurred to her that the managers in her mentor's department were not promoted into leadership roles. Why was that? After talking with others and thinking it through, Crystal decided that her ''model'' had not demonstrated enough leadership. He was a solid manager, but did not take the risks necessary in becoming a leader.

As a result, Crystal switched models. She discovered Ms. Crane, who was both a strong leader and manager. Crystal became more visible and more decisive in her communications. She used all three of her power sources. In talking it over with her husband, Crystal said, ''I just decided that I had to start acting like a leader if I wanted future upward mobility.''

Is this typical of a situation in your organization? Are excellent managers often left in their roles? Is it necessary to become a leader/manager to gain upward mobility? Defend your position in the spaces below and then compare your answer with those of the author's on page 74.

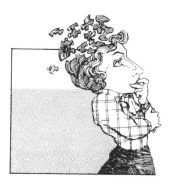

CRYSTAL PUT THE PIECES TOGETHER

NOTES

SUMMARY: BALANCING YOUR POWER SOURCES

Naturally, the more personality power you develop the stronger your role as a leader can be. You will be able to communicate better. You will be more convincing when you ask others to accept your vision. Your stronger personality will help you convert more employees into followers.

But it is not always how much power you have. More important is how you employ it. Sensitivity to others is the key! And sensitivity is facilitated when personality power is balanced with both role power and knowledge power. Many variables are involved.

A leader with great knowledge can be effective even with a minimum of personality power.

A leader who downplays role power and makes the most of his or her knowledge power can be effective with just modest personality power.

A leader with little role power and in a position where knowledge power is not highly important, is dependent upon personality power.

In summary, the following suggestions are made:

- Everyone has a few features (often physical) that others appreciate. Play your winners!

- Strive to develop all of the best mental traits that are expected in leaders, but feature a few that are most important to you so they will be talked about in a favorable light by others.

- Be proud of your personality and keep in mind that those who do not transmit their personalities effectively often look better to others than they do to themselves.

- Use the magic of a positive attitude to enhance your personality.

- Use caution in selecting the best possible leadership model.

NOTES

P A R T

IV

Develop
A Vision

LEADERS KNOW WHERE THEY ARE GOING

Think of the leaders you admire and you will usually find something unique about them. Great leaders inspire people to follow more than just "mind the store." Status quo is not enough: Leaders are on the move, improving, growing, and expanding into new areas.

What further distinguishes leaders is that their growth has a direction. Leaders know where they are going. As a follower, you might be charting new territory with your leader. The process is exciting. A key ingredient is that leaders have a vision to which they are drawn.

To be a true leader, you must have a sense of what's important, how you can contribute, and make a mark. What do you value and how can you make those values contribute in a larger sense? If your ultimate aims are based upon self interest, employees are not going to be highly motivated to the extra mile. On the other hand, if your team can see how your direction can make a difference, their energy and focus will support your goals.

At times managers will say, "There is no way I can shape my department. That's done by those above me." In the end, however, it is either create your future or let others do it. Recall the leaders you admire. They didn't accept the status quo. Chances are they pushed, nudged, and changed the way things were previously done.

Once you begin to get a picture of your larger goal or vision, you can begin to strategize. The focus is more on the "how" rather than the "what." A word of caution. In the past decade or two, we have glorified quantitative decision making. This has led some to focus a disproportional amount of attention on the correct calculations. Your vision cannot be determined with a calculator or a case study. It must be what matters most to you. There are no rights or wrongs when it comes to a vision, just what is passionately important to you.

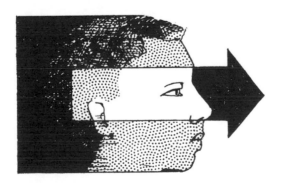

CASE STUDY 2:

TOO MUCH ATTENTION TO DETAIL?

Barbara has always taken a great deal of professional pride in her accounting skills. She was a top student at school and has excelled in her job. In recognition of her performance, Barbara was named accounting manager.

Barbara's attention to detail was always one of her greatest assets. Now that she is in management, the details of her position have increased tenfold, and she feels as if she is drowning. Her greatest asset has become a liability!

To get a handle on things, Barbara has tried making lists. But there aren't enough hours to deal with everything on her lists. To make matters worse, her boss has begun to ask questions about where she's ''taking her department'' and what's her ''focus.''

Barbara is beginning to wonder if she is really cut out for leadership. Is there hope?

Write out your response below and compare with that found on page 74.

MY LISTS SEEM TO KEEP GROWING!

SEE THE PATTERNS— DELEGATE THE DETAILS

To truly lead a group, you must not lose sight of the long view. You need to see the patterns, trends, and opportunities rather than get caught up in the details, particularly when these immediate details loom as roadblocks. If you are true to your dream, your roadblocks will become hurdles.

Some Strategies for Staying Focused

1. *No Details Until 10:00 a.m.* Many managers work best in the morning, but often find that this time is consumed by small issues. To stay focused on their larger goals, some managers set a rule that they are not to be interrupted and no meetings are to be scheduled until 10:00 a.m. During this time, they shut their door and get the meat of their serious work underway.

2. *Your Top Six.* Mary Kay Ashe, Chief Executive Officer of Mary Kay Cosmetics, gets her focus set at the end of each day. Before she leaves work, she writes down the six most important activities for the next day. When she comes in the next morning, these six items are handled first, before she gets pulled into the daily details.

3. *Assess Your Focus.* Think about yesterday. What percentage of your time was spent moving toward your vision and long-term goals, and what percentage dealt with the daily drama of life? Balance is the key!

WHERE ARE DECISIONS TAKING YOUR DEPARTMENT?

Make sure you take the long view, particularly in important decisions. It is important for you as a leader to demonstrate focus and consistency. Underlying these qualities are your values, and how you see yourself contributing to your department, organization, or industry. For example, regardless of responsibility, a leader wants a product with the most integrity, the highest quality, the safest reputation, the most dependability, etc. In other words, the desire to be the best is a passion.

This value focus drives decisions. There is no compromise. As a leader you may need to sacrifice a short term goal to stay true to your vision. Do it! Nothing is more important than the big picture.

Consistency in where you are leading your followers is extremely important. Employees find it hard to keep that extra level of motivation if decisions indicate they are headed one way today and another direction tomorrow. The consistency of your decisions signals your commitment to what you believe to be important.

Following is an excellent summary of a decision process outlined in *Successful Self-Management* that can be ordered using the form in the back of this book.

1. Make the best decision you can—BY DOING IT—and then observe your results.

2. Avoid ''perfection paralysis.'' Everything you do won't be perfect, but if you start with a ''rough draft'' and then shape and improve things as you go, you'll end up fine. Keep the big picture in mind.

3. Use a decision guide like the one illustrated below.

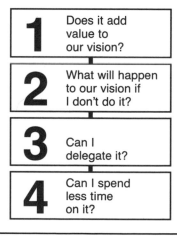

1 Does it add value to our vision?

2 What will happen to our vision if I don't do it?

3 Can I delegate it?

4 Can I spend less time on it?

CASE STUDY 3:

PRESSURE FROM ABOVE

Miranda is the customer service manager in a large organization and her employees are about to mutiny. Two weeks ago in her staff meeting, she told them that senior management was very concerned about the labor budget. Employees had to up their number of calls. No excuses would be allowed. Productivity was the only goal.

Her employees took her to heart. They processed more customer calls than ever. Customers' complaint calls skyrocketed. Customers complained that they weren't listened to, were cut off during mid-sentence, and more. Now Miranda is saying that customer service is more important than productivity.

This morning she has announced that the quarterly report is due in a week—and that it is now top priority. Her employees don't know what is most important or where to focus their energy.

How would you counsel Miranda if you were her superior?

Compare with suggested answer an page 74.

MIRANDA'S EMPLOYEES ARE SKEPTICAL!

PUTTING YOUR VISION INTO ACTION

To this point, we've looked at some of the major components of leadership. Now it's time to put these concepts into some concrete steps. You may be clear on your vision, but it's often difficult for employees to see its relationship to daily activities, understand their part in it, or even how to support the vision without working at cross purposes with you.

The process for turning ideas into reality is communication, both verbal and written. Leaders are clear about the goals they set for themselves and for their followers.

Let's first look at where you stand with respect to leadership skills. Read the statement in both columns and then place a ☑ in the appropriate square.

☐ I plan long-term.	☐ I focus on getting through the day or week.
☐ I determine what direction my teams should take.	☐ I wait for direction from above.
☐ I focus on how my area of responsibility serves the organization and our customers.	☐ I focus on what my department is supposed to do.
☐ I share my vision with employees and help guide their work.	☐ Employees know what to do. They have their day-to-day assignments.
☐ I look at what is needed for my personal growth.	☐ I'm too busy to worry about personal growth and development.
☐ My employees are clear about how to be a success in their job.	☐ My employees are happy doing what they do.
☐ I consciously manage and shape change in my department.	☐ Changes occur and there is little I can do about them.
☐ I plan for the growth and development of my employees.	☐ We're too busy around here for personal growth and development.
☐ I encourage my employees to try new methods.	☐ I would rather my employees use the tried and true methods of doing their work.
☐ We celebrate personal and departmental successes.	☐ We keep our noses to the grindstone.

If you checked more boxes in the left column, you're on your way to becoming a leader.

COMMUNICATING A VISION

Leaders generate excitement, interest and energy in others. And they do this through communication. How you talk about your vision will determine how much others will want to mentally "sign up" to follow you.

Two keys in how you speak about your vision are: Consistency and repetition. First, let's consider consistency. If you notice, leaders are usually eager to describe their vision and do it in a rather predictable way. This isn't because they lack creativity. It is because their vision doesn't change from day-to-day. What leaders focus on is how the future will look as a result of their vision. They describe the benefits inherent in their vision and their personal belief in its importance.

A vision is not a set speech given from notes at formal occasions. Rather, it appears to be impromptu and delivered to anyone who will listen. If you want others to follow you, you've got to get out there and describe where you're going. The consistency becomes important so that others will get a clear picture of where you're taking them.

Sometimes managers find communicating a vision difficult. It's more comfortable to stay in the office and do a job. That's not leadership! If you have ever heard Steve Jobs, one of the co-founders of Apple Computers, speak about his vision you realize how infectious he can be. Jobs is very soft-spoken, but he gets people excited about the future, even if they can't understand computers!

The second part of the process is repetition. Once isn't enough. This month isn't enough. Your communication must be continuous and repetitive. Initially people will wonder if you are serious or is this the "flavor of the month." After people hear the message frequently enough and see that your behaviors are consistent with your message then, and only then, will they begin to believe you are serious. When they know you are determined, they will also begin to believe in your vision.

An added plus to frequency is focus. If you keep talking about your vision, you won't lose sight of the target.

WORKING WITH STAKEHOLDERS

Although it is fine to communicate your vision to anyone who will listen, you will also need to target selected individuals and groups. These people are called stakeholders.

Stakeholders are those who can help or hinder you in attaining your vision because they have something at stake. Certainly this includes your employees and boss. But others are also important, such as your peers, managers of other departments, senior management, peers outside the organization, or your family, to name just a few. On the help side, stakeholders are people who can provide you with information, ideas, finances, a good word, or even emotional support. On the hinder side, they may be individuals who see your ideas as threatening to their power, security, or people who support the status quo.

If you are strategic, you need to know who these people are. Take a minute to begin jotting down some names or initials.

Likely to Help	Likely to Hinder
_____	_____
_____	_____
_____	_____
_____	_____
_____	_____

If some of your stakeholders are people you don't normally see in your day-to-day business, you may need to create opportunities to chat with them about your vision. These could include:

- Invite stakeholders to your department meeting.
- Stop by their office.
- Ask their advice about an idea or problem.
- Take them to lunch.
- Send them a book or article.
- Invite them to serve on a committee.
- Involve them in a planning session.
- Add your own:

_____

_____

YOU NEED SPECIFIC GOALS TO REACH YOUR VISION

Your vision is your picture of the future. It is global and not precise. It is critical to have a vision, but a vision alone is not enough. You also need to create specific goals to reach your vision. Goals have a more limited time horizon. Some leaders write yearly goals; others are more comfortable writing goals on a six-month basis. Choose whatever time horizon seems most comfortable to you.

Think of your vision as where you'd like to go. Think of your goals as the specifics about how to get there. It is important to write both visions and goals down. But goals, in order to work, must have some specific built-in components.

How to Write Goals that Work:

1. Be SPECIFIC. Identify either the exact outcome you want or the process (how much by when).

2. Make goals MEASURABLE. How will you measure whether you've been successful or not? Where is your goal line and how will you know if you've crossed it?

3. Goals must be REASONABLE. Sometimes in our exuberance over an idea, we set goals which are impossible to reach. Make sure your goals are humanly possible given your present demands.

4. Finally, goals must be TIME SPECIFIC. Not ''as soon as I can,'' but, ''by May 23rd.''

An important aspect of this goal-setting process is NOT to get bogged down in paperwork or write a goal for everything. Be strategic. What are the most important targets you must hit to achieve your vision? Three to five may be appropriate, never more than eight. Some examples follow.

SAMPLE GOALS

''Institute a customer service survey by January 5th. This survey will be mailed to all of our customers each quarter. The survey will inquire about: 1) quality of the product; 2) delivery time; and 3) assistance provided on the 800 telephone number. Results from the survey will be compiled and presented at the quarterly planning meeting.''

''Increase our department's total sales volume this year over last year's by 17% by year's end. This goal assures maintaining the present level of customer satisfaction as measured by our Customer Satisfaction Report.''

''Design an office layout for the new offices by October 15th. The layout will include workstations for all employees, and fulfillment space that allows for a thirty percent addition to the present area.''

SET SOME GOALS
BEFORE THIS WEEKEND

It is time to try writing your goals. What do you want to accomplish in the next year or sooner to move toward your vision?

My major goals are:

	Is This Goal:			
	Specific?	Measurable?	Reasonable?	Time Specific?
GOAL 1)				
2)				
3)				
4)				
5)				

Note: Goals can never be set in concrete; organizations are too dynamic. This process is your best assessment at the time, and will probably have to change to some degree during the year.

Also, you may want to involve your employees in the goal-setting process. Employees who are new to the organization and in training may find it difficult to contribute. On the other hand, they may find it enlightening.

P A R T

V

Making Better And Faster Decisions

EENIE
MEENIE
MYNIE
MOE

DECISION MAKING FOR LEADERS

Once you have established a larger goal or vision, how quickly you move forward will be shaped by the decisions you make. Our success or failure is usually based upon the quality of our decisions.

Four important components of leadership decisions are:

Being True to Your Vision: Where It Will Take You.
Your vision is your beacon, your guiding light. It underlies all your decisions and gives your leadership consistency. Employees may not agree with all of your decisions, but if they see the consistency behind them, they can support and follow.

How: The Formula. When we have dozens of decisions every day, it is very easy to "shoot from the hip," rather than analyzing the situation. A few important steps in decision making can improve your product and/or service.

When: Analysis Paralysis. The information age has brought thousands of facts to our fingertips. You might think this leads to a better decision, but the opposite is often the case. The sheer amount of data can lead to analysis paralysis. Leaders must know how to make decisions without pouring over every bit of data.

Who: Decisions at the Right Level. Nothing can bog a leader down more quickly than trying to make all the decisions. It is not easy to delegate decisions to others who might not be as knowledgeable. And it can be confusing as to which decisions are yours. Most important in delegating decisions is strategically choosing which to delegate and then consistently delegating those to others.

USING A FORMULA FOR DECISION MAKING

Some decisions are simple and the answers are obvious. Others are complex, and require you to weigh a variety of factors. At times, it's not even clear what the problems or issues are that have to be solved.

Having a formula to help you to sort through a decision can help you look at factors and identify your best options.

The formula below is designed to help make decision making more methodical.

Process	Instructions
1. Define desired outcome.	You need to know exactly what you want to accomplish before you can decide the best way to do it.
2. Establish decision criteria.	What are the guideposts? For example, if you were deciding whether to drive or take the bus to work, you would consider factors like safety, cost, or time saved.
3. Come up with alternative solutions.	Write out all possible courses of action that will lead to the desired outcome.
4. Investigate—get all possible facts.	Accumulate as many facts as time permits. List them on a separate sheet of paper.
5. Settle on top three choices.	List them.
6. Instigate a comparison	Weigh the three choices and decide among them. Consult with others if necessary.
7. Opt for the best choice.	List your final decision.
8. Notify those involved with decisiveness.	The way you articulate your decision can be as important as the quality of the decision itself. Write how you intend to announce it.
9. See that decision is fully implemented.	A good decision must be made to work. Write out how you intend to do this.

KNOWING WHEN TO HOLD AND WHEN TO FOLD

Timing is another significant element in your leadership tool box. Obviously you want to make the best possible decision in the most efficient way. Some managers demand all the financial data, historical information, power-brokers' opinions, customer feedback, and more. Unfortunately, by the time all this data is gathered, it is either too late or overwhelming. The results are inconsistent. This type of situation leads to poor decisions at best, and paralysis at worst.

So how do you make decisions if you can't know everything? First, as a leader, you must stay current and focused on the trends in your industry, organization and/or department. You need to look for patterns of growth, opportunities, and problems. Leaders are continuously working to anticipate the future rather than react to it. Certainly there may be some data you must have or some individuals (such as your boss) whose support is absolutely necessary. But the challenge of leadership is judging when you have enough information so you are not shooting from the hip, and not waiting so long that the strategic moment to take advantage of the situation has passed. Leaders often talk about making "gut" decisions. Although this may sound unusual, what they are really talking about is understanding the patterns without getting lost in the data.

A reality of decision making is that you will at times make the wrong decision. Yes, if you had waited longer, this would have become obvious. Consider it a lesson in your school of leadership. You won't do it perfectly every time. Fifty-one percent of making the right decision is a step in the right direction.

FREEING YOURSELF TO LEAD

The "who" of decision making is an essential factor. You can't be a true leader sensing the environment for trends and focusing on the long haul if you are bogged down in the daily detail of decision making. If employees need to come to you for every "OK," the decision-making process must be pushed to a lower level.

Consider how many decisions, large and small, you make in a day. Could or should others be shouldering part of this load? Often managers are reluctant to let go of decision making. Following are some of the common reasons. Check those you feel are true of you.

☐   I can decide faster.

☐   I would be out of control if I'm not making the decisions.

☐   I know all the factors; my employees don't.

☐   The employee might make a mistake.

☐   I have more experience and therefore can make better decisions.

☐   I feel guilty asking the employee to make the decision when it's my responsibility.

☐   My employees don't like making decisions and want me to decide.

☐   I like making all the decisions.

If any of the above sound like you, it's time to change. You can't be a leader if you are involved in every day-to-day decision. If you feel your employees are unprepared to handle decisions on their own, then it is time to prepare them. If they don't have the background, make sure they get it. If they don't have the confidence, work with them. Praise their good decisions. If they tend to put it back on your plate, consistently give the decision back. Leaders cannot be involved in the daily load of details.

Where you must focus your decision making energy is on those issues that set the direction of your responsibilities. You must be at the forefront in any decision that will have a long-term impact.

CASE STUDY 4:

CARLOS CAN'T DECIDE

Carlos dreamed of the day he would become a manager. He looked forward to calling the shots and making the decisions. Carlos and his company enjoy a sophisticated management information system that can provide reports, data, projections, and the history of just about every product imaginable to help him make the right decisions.

Much to his surprise, Carlos finds his stomach in knots when it's time to decide. He wonders if there is another way to look at the data. Should he ask for an additional report? Should he talk to finance? Should he do more research? Should he read another article? He wants to make the right decision, and suddenly it seems as if there is no right decision.

Lately, Carlos has noticed that his employees seem to be kidding him about whether decisions have been made yet. Even his boss has made some remarks. The problem is, he's just not sure yet if there are other factors to be considered.

What would you counsel Carlos to do? See author's response on page 74.

CARLOS LOOKS AT THE DATA

PORTRAIT
OF A DECISION

You may remember the Tylenol poisoning scare that happened several years ago. People who had taken Tylenol were dying and no one knew why. James Burke, the Chief Executive Officer of Johnson & Johnson, faced one of the toughest decisions of his life. Should he pull Tylenol from all the stores?

The financial cost would be enormous. The legal implications could be staggering. His decision was—pull the product.

Burke attributes his decision to the values underlying his company, Johnson & Johnson's credo which begins, ''We believe our first responsibility is to the doctors, nurses and patients, to mothers and all others who use our products and services.'' Burke is a clear example of a leader who knew his values and used them to make decisions. Additionally, he kept the long view in focus. Yes, J&J suffered financially that year, but they came back stronger than ever with more customer trust than they could have bought with millions of dollars in advertising.

DEVELOPING YOUR DECISION-MAKING SKILLS

Read the statement at both ends of the scale and then circle the number that best indicates where you belong.

	HIGH	LOW	
When making an important decision I consider how it fits my vision.	10 9 8 7 6 5 4 3 2 1		It's too difficult to consider my vision when making important decisions.
My followers see consistency in my decisions.	10 9 8 7 6 5 4 3 2 1		There's very little consistency in my decisions.
I feel comfortable making a decision without all related data.	10 9 8 7 6 5 4 3 2 1		I must have as much data as possible to make a decision.
I am careful not to overwhelm myself with information when making a decision.	10 9 8 7 6 5 4 3 2 1		I often feel overwhelmed by the data when making a decision.
I am able to make timely decisions.	10 9 8 7 6 5 4 3 2 1		I procrastinate when decisions are important.
I communicate my decision to those who will be impacted.	10 9 8 7 6 5 4 3 2 1		I neglect or forget to tell people about decisions that may impact them.
I stay up-to-date with industry and organization trends.	10 9 8 7 6 5 4 3 2 1		I'm too busy to worry about industry and organization trends.
I delegate decisions to employees that they can and should make.	10 9 8 7 6 5 4 3 2 1		I make most of the decisions.
I am committed to developing my employees so they can make more and better decisions.	10 9 8 7 6 5 4 3 2 1		My employees would prefer me to make the decisions.
When a decision is complex, I follow a logical formula.	10 9 8 7 6 5 4 3 2 1		When a decision is complex, I muddle through as best I can.

SCORE ☐

If you scored 100-90, you are an outstanding decision maker on all important fronts. If you scored 89-80, you are very good at decision making and involve the appropriate individuals. If you scored 79-70, you are doing well, but may want to look at the answers you checked for areas you can improve upon even more. If you scored below 70, you may want to develop a decision-making improvement plan.

TAKING CARE OF YOUR PERSONAL GROWTH

A serious oversight some managers make is not attending to their personal leadership growth. Just as with developing employees, what you know and do today won't be sufficient for the rapidly changing business environment. You can't let personal growth slide until you "have the time." That time will never come. You must have a development plan for yourself. If you don't write it down, another "crisis" will take priority. Take a moment to assess your development needs and then take appropriate action.

What I Need to Know?	How I'm Going to Learn It?	By When?
(For example: The latest trends in my industry.	Attend an association meeting at which an industry forecaster is speaking.	Dec., 19____)

HELPING YOUR STAFF GROW

People normally fall into two groups: Those who create their future, and those who let others create it. Leaders are solidly in the former group.

Leaders are never satisfied with the status quo. They are always looking for ways to ''do things better than we are doing them today.'' True leaders seem to brim with new ideas. These ideas come from constant scanning of the environment for trends and direction. But the focus on improvement isn't just products or services—it's also the people.

As a leader, an important message to your followers is that everyone, regardless of experience or job title, should be constantly improving. Daily work becomes an ongoing classroom. Some ways to foster personal improvement include:

- Attend formal outside workshops and seminars.

- Work directly with employees to share insights.

- Devise group projects for cross training.

- Visit other organizations or departments.

- Develop or attend in-house training courses.

- Encourage special projects which enhance skills and abilities.

- Read books, journals and articles.

One company president holds a monthly book review meeting with her key managers. The president selects one book a month related to business. All read the book and then discuss which ideas are appropriate for their business.

Whatever avenue you use, the message you send when you encourage growth is that you encourage people to expand their skills and knowledge.

Crisp Publications, Inc. has an entire series of self-help books. For more information, see the listing in the back of this book.

NOTES

PART

VI

Taking More Risks

THE MILLION DOLLAR GOOF

The president of Acme Manufacturing called and asked to see Bob. Bob knows why the president called and wonders if it is time to update his resume.

Bob is the manager of new product development. For the past year he has been working on a special product. So far the company has spent more than a million dollars in the development, production, and preliminary marketing of this new product.

The product has been on the market for three months and first quarter sales have just been reported. The product appears to be a total bomb with no hope of selling anywhere near its projection. That's a million dollars down the drain and Bob was one of those primarily responsible.

Bob entered the president's office fearing it would be the end of his career at Acme. Although he contributed a lot to the company over the years, a million dollars is a million dollars. To speed things along, Bob told the president, "I know why you asked to see me. I understand your position. You'll have my resignation by the end of the day."

The president interrupted Bob by saying, "Slow down. We all have to make educated guesses when making decisions. I'm sure you learned a lot from this product launch. I can't affort to lose you. We just spent a million dollars on your education."

1. What do you think the president gained from the approach?

2. How do you think this will affect Bob's future performance?

BOB'S MILLION DOLLAR LESSON

LEARNING FROM FAILURES

Whenever we change how we are doing things, expect some problems. Whenever we make a change, we are taking a risk. This is not necessarily bad; in fact, progress comes from applying new ideas to old problems. Leaders are risk takers. As they forge into the unknown looking for a better way, they may stumble, meet a roadblock, or fail.

As a leader, you obviously don't want to take unwarranted risks. But it would be far more damaging to take no risks. Calculated risks are part and parcel of leadership.

What is important is how you deal with your failure should one of your risks backfire. Some managers allow failure to damage their self-esteem. As a result, these individuals are less likely to take future risks and the process can become a downward career spiral. Managers who only do what is safe—will not become leaders. The focus during failure needs to be on what has been learned. Leaders see risk taking and failure as an opportunity to learn valuable lessons.

List three failures resulting from risks you took and write what you learned from each experience. Use more paper if necessary.

Failure	Lessons Learned
1.	1.
2.	2.
3.	3.

Were these failures valuable learning experiences for you?

YES ☐   NO ☐

RISK ANALYSIS EXERCISE

Often we are reluctant to take a risk because of various imagined negative consequences. But we are usually vague about what those consequences actually would be. If we realistically identify the worst possible outcome, it isn't all that bad.

To overcome this, you might try the following exercise. You can do this with either a risk you are considering or one that one of your employees is reluctant to try.

STEP 1.   Describe the potential risk: _____

_____

_____

_____

STEP 2. Describe the worst possible outcome.
(Note: Be specific. Not "It would be just awful," or "I'd look like a fool," but "The report would be a day late," or "Sue would think I hadn't tried.")

_____

_____

_____

_____

_____

STEP 3. Now list the benefits if the risk is a success.

_____

_____

_____

_____

_____

STEP 4. On balance, is it worth taking the risk? _____ Yes _____ No

LEADERS CAN EFFECTIVELY MANAGE CHANGE

As your vision takes shape on the job, things will naturally begin to change. Most of us are to some degree uncomfortable with change. Some recognize the benefit of doing business differently and take advantage of opportunities. At the other extreme, others will wail, ''We tried that back in '72 and it doesn't work!''

As a leader, when you encounter resistance, you must manage change strategically. To assist you, there are three major tools in your ''change management tool chest.'' They are: Reward, comfort in the new way, and replay optimism. Following are the three primary ways to deal with the resistance to change you will inevitably encounter.

1. *Providing Payoffs.*

Payoffs or rewards can be extremely effective in bringing about change. Given the change you would like followers to master, what payoffs can you provide when the change occurs? How can you make it rewarding when your follower takes the risk of trying something new? You can't wait until followers are 100% behind the change, or they may never get there. Instead, when you see an employee begin to accept the change, you need to praise and acknowledge the attempt, even if it's not wholehearted or done perfectly. What this means is, you are providng a payoff to make it worth going through the change.

2. *Greasing the Skids.*

The second tool is to make change more comfortable. How can you make the status quo undesirable so that the employee would rather make the change? You may change things so that it takes more time or effort to do it the old way. Or you might remove approval or other social awards that the employee previously received. Often group pressure such as joking or kidding, can help some of the most entrenched change old ways.

3. *Assuring with Optimism.*

Some people are extremely fearful of change. They can only see the down side. As a leader you need to help this person see the benefits of the change. You can do this with reassuring optimism. You should consistently state your belief in the worth, impact, possibility, etc., of the change. You don't let the change resisters pull you down with their negativism. If the resister says, ''Top management will never support it,'' the optimistic reply is, ''I think once we've presented our ideas, they will be behind us.'' State what you plan to gain the needed support.

Let's look at a case.

CHANGE EXERCISE

Neil, one of your employees, is responsible for putting together the company's monthly newsletter. This takes a large portion of his time and Neil is justly very proud of his product. Virtually everyone in the company knows Neil because of the newsletter, and he's often acknowledged formally and informally because he does such a good job.

Recently, you've become aware of desktop publishing. After seeing a demonstration, you couldn't wait to tell Neil about the possibilities. When you told Neil about it, he immediately threw up verbal barriers. He said using a computer instead of doing everything by hand would take away the creative process which now makes the newsletter so outstanding.

What could you do in each of these areas: (List your responses below.)

PROVIDING PAYOFFS. _____

_____

_____

_____

_____

GREASING THE SKIDS. _____

_____

_____

_____

_____

ASSURING WITH OPTIMISM: _____

_____

_____

_____

_____

(Match your responses with those of the author's on the next page. Your responses do not have to be identical with those of the authors, but should convey the same spirit.)

MATCH YOUR RESPONSE

(AUTHOR SUGGESTED RESPONSES)

PROVIDING PAYOFFS

a) If Neil uses the computer for part of the newsletter, praise him.

b) Offer him the opportunity to attend a ''desktop publishing'' seminar.

c) Discuss with him the opportunities to link up with others such as graphics specialists to obtain more and better input for the newsletters.

d) Mention any positive feedback you have heard about his attempts at new or different techniques.

e) Identify newsletters he admires from other organizations and have him visit those organizations, on company time, to research the techniques they are using.

GREASING THE SKIDS

a) Move Neil's layout equipment to the back room and put the computer in its place.

b) Stop commenting on the newsletter.

c) Create performance goals related to automation of the newsletter.

d) Give him an assignment that would more easily or professionally be done with desktop publishing.

e) Limit amount of time he can spend on the newsletter.

f) Introduce others in the organization to desktop publishing so they question Neil about his expertise in this area.

ASSURING WITH OPTIMISM

State your beliefs about:

a) The professional new look desktop publishing will give the newsletter.

b) Neil's ability to transition to desktop publishing.

c) The support you've heard from top management.

(In general, when Neil comments on why it won't work, you state your belief about how it will work.)

THE SAFE ROAD TO NOWHERE

How you handle the failures of followers is equally as important as how you handle personal failures. So often, a manager will cajole, coax, and beg a follower to be creative and experiment with new methods. They see employee resistance as just stubbornness. What this manager may fail to take into account is that in the past, when the followers *did* try something new and it failed, the follower had a negative experience from the manager. This type of experience encourages taking the safe road in the future.

An example of a typical change-frustration was an executive who managed thirty service businesses in five states. He once said about the managers running the businesses, ''I keep talking to them about needing to change but nothing changes. Sometimes I just want to shake them.'' What this executive failed to take into account was that unsuccessful change attempts in the past had brought swift negative responses from corporate. What the executive saw as good management on his part, his managers saw as a problem. His people weren't dumb, they were simply protecting themselves.

If you want change, you cannot punish reasonable risks. You may even want to reward a failure if the risk was well conceived and one to be admired. If you let your employees know that you understand the rationale for doing what was done and that you appreciate his or her effort, you will probably have two results: 1) a surprised employee, and 2) someone ready to risk change in the future.

HERE ARE SOME PERFECTLY
GOOD REASONS TO CHANGE!

NOTES

P A R T

VII

Summary

MANAGEMENT/LEADERSHIP ASSESSMENT SCALE

This survey describes twenty (20) practices that are commonly demonstrated by excellent managers and twenty (20) commonly demonstrated by effective leaders. Please read all statements carefully. Then decide as a manager/leader the priority you would assign each practice or characteristic. Indicate your decision by circling the appropriate number.

	PRIORITY				
	Highest	High	Important	Modest	Low
1. Gets tough when needed.	5	4	3	2	1
2. Speaks well to groups.	5	4	3	2	1
3. Establishes consistent, clear displine line.	5	4	3	2	1
4. Attracts others to message that is given.	5	4	3	2	1
5. Provides environment conducive to a feeling of cohesiveness.	5	4	3	2	1
6. Communicates sense of ''being in charge.''	5	4	3	2	1
7. Has full backing from those reporting to her/him.	5	4	3	2	1
8. Converts employees into followers.	5	4	3	2	1
9. Strives to win by allowing employees to also win.	5	4	3	2	1
10. Attracts others to join his/her group.	5	4	3	2	1
11. Provides important rewards to staff.	5	4	3	2	1
12. Utilizes sources of power in a sensitive, consistent manager.	5	4	3	2	1

CONTINUED PAGES 66 AND 67

MANAGEMENT/LEADERSHIP ASSESSMENT SCALE (Continued)

	Highest	High	Important	Modest	Low
			PRIORITY		
13. Shows compassion.	5	4	3	2	1
14. Strong track record for making solid and decisive decisions.	5	4	3	2	1
15. Good listener.	5	4	3	2	1
16. Formalizes and "stages" communication announcements.	5	4	3	2	1
17. Expresses thoughts clearly.	5	4	3	2	1
18. Prudent risk taker.	5	4	3	2	1
19. Keeps employees fully informed.	5	4	3	2	1
20. Articulates an inspiring mission.	5	4	3	2	1
21. Highly ethical.	5	4	3	2	1
22. Generates a feeling of pride in followers.	5	4	3	2	1
23. Delegates effectively.	5	4	3	2	1
24. Ties short-term work goals to mission.	5	4	3	2	1
25. Shares large and small victories with staff.	5	4	3	2	1
26. Gets others caught up in his/her positive force.	5	4	3	2	1
27. Makes work enjoyable.	5	4	3	2	1
28. Creates active tempo.	5	4	3	2	1
29. Maintains positive, upbeat attitude.	5	4	3	2	1

	PRIORITY				
	Highest	**High**	**Important**	**Modest**	**Low**
30. Highly energetic; not "desk bound."	5	4	3	2	1
31. Admits to mistakes.	5	4	3	2	1
32. Good negotiator; knows when to compromise.	5	4	3	2	1
33. Follows logical steps in making decisions.	5	4	3	2	1
34. If she/he resigned, others would consider following.	5	4	3	2	1
35. Consults with others in making decisions.	5	4	3	2	1
36. Builds commitment to his/her cause.	5	4	3	2	1
37. Uses management role with sensitivity.	5	4	3	2	1
38. Stands firm on principle.	5	4	3	2	1
39. Respected by employees when authority is used.	5	4	3	2	1
40. Communicates a power image.	5	4	3	2	1

All of the above practices that are found in effective *managers* have odd numbers. Those practices not always found in managers but *usually found in leaders* have even numbers.

Please add up all the numbers circled in the *odd* numbered statements and enter into this box:

Management Practices

Please add up all the numbers circled in the *even* numbered statements and enter into this box:

Leadership Practices

SEE NEXT PAGE
FOR INTERPRETATION

POSSIBLE INTERPRETATION

1. If the score in the Management Practices box on page 67 is higher than the score on page 11, it is an indication that becoming more familiar with Leadership Practices may improve your status as a manager either now or later.

2. If the score in the Leadership Practices box is 80 or above, it would appear you are getting a signal that you are ''ready'' to take on a stronger leadership role.

3. If the score in the Leadership Practices box is between 60 and 80, it may be a signal that you are ''getting ready'' to move into a leadership role.

4. If your Leadership Practices score is substantially under your Management Practices score, it may be an indication that leadership, at this time, may not be for you.

5. Please list any additional interpretations that you make from the results of your assessments.

_____

_____

_____

_____

_____

MONDAY'S REALITY
A Leadership Maintenance Kit

Like having your car serviced regularly, the purpose of this one-page KIT is to remind you to do maintenance on your leadership skills. Check those that need to be activated Monday morning.

☐ Keeping the "positive force" created last week alive?

☐ Giving new rewards to staff?

☐ Solve any carry-over problems decisively?

☐ Restore the vision previously painted?

☐ Be a better example than last week?

☐ Establish a more upbeat tempo?

☐ Laugh at yourself more frequently?

☐ Keep management skills sharp so you will continue to have more time to lead?

☐ Make others feel better about their decision to follow you?

☐ Make better use of power sources?

☐ Do a better job of holding emotions in check?

☐ Communicate a stronger, more positive attitude?

☐ If goals are met by Thursday, relax with staff and share the victory on Friday?

☐ Spend more time teaching others?

☐ Show a stronger bearing through the way you walk, talk, and listen?

☐ Take more risks?

☐ Make faster, better decisions?

DEVELOPING YOUR LEADERSHIP SKILLS

If you've chosen to develop your leadership skills, you probably have a number of specific skills you feel are important to strengthen. As we've talked about in this book, it's often easy to get caught in daily crises and lose sight of long-term objectives.

Take a few minutes right now to do some planning for your own leadership development. What area(s) would you like to focus on developing in the next two to three months?

☐ personality power   ☐ managing change

☐ my vision   ☐ developing stakeholders

☐ speaking skills   ☐ long-term goal setting

☐ delegation   ☐ decision making

☐ risk taking   ☐ other

DEVELOPING YOUR LEADERSHIP VISION

A true leader is constantly developing his/her skills. You have probably identified some leadership skills you would like to develop. You may wonder where to begin. A good idea is to first list the skills you wish to improve. Then prioritize which you plan to attack first (give those an "A"). Those that are important, but are not top priority should be labeled "B". Any remaining can be labeled "C".

Leadership Tools to Develop:

The second step in this process is to identify a few leaders you feel are top-notch models, and whom you have an opportunity to observe.

Leaders to Observe:

The next step is to make a conscious effort to observe these leaders and how they use the tools you are developing. Even better is to "pick their brains" and get some leadership coaching.

Ideas from Leaders:

The final step is to create your own model of leadership. What are the qualities you feel are critical in order to be the best leader you can possibly be?

My Leadership Model:

CASE STUDY 5:

TO LEAD OR NOT TO LEAD

Robin has been a supervisor for six months. She has become a good administrator, and does what is required of her in the position.

Recently, Robin has been reading in the area of leadership and found herself admiring individuals with these qualities. As Robin began to consider developing her own leadership abilities, she realized that such an endeavor would not be easy. She would have to take a hard look at her strengths and weaknesses and really put some work into self-development.

Robin is torn. The position only "requires" that she be effective in her administrative duties, which won't necessitate any additional work on her part. However, Robin also sees an opportunity to make a difference as a leader, but that's going to require some real commitment to her own development.

Which choice is right for Robin? Compare your answer with that of the authors on the next page.

ROBIN READY TO LEAD HER TEAM?

SUGGESTED ANSWERS TO CASE STUDIES

Case Study 1: Crystal made a smart move in switching role models. Some organizations develop many good managers but few leaders. In these firms, managers usually stay in their present positions longer. In almost all organizations, leadership is the key to greater upward mobility.

Case Study 2: Barbara's dilemma is far more common than she realizes. Employees who receive many accolades for meticulously taking care of details find the move to management and leadership exceptionally painful. It is time for Barbara to refocus. She needs to develop her vision and long-term goals. She needs to see the patterns and trends in her department, organization, and industry. If she stays in her world of detail (her choice) her upward mobility is limited.

Case Study 3: Miranda, confused by Senior Management, is sending mixed signals to her staff. As a result, they are frustrated and critical of her leadership. Miranda needs to give her followers one clear, understandable direction even if this means acting as a ''buffer and interpreter'' of what she is receiving from above.

Case Study 4: Carlos needs to design a decision-making formula that is comfortable for him to use—one in which he can have confidence. After doing this, he needs to remind himself that: (1) All decisions are calculated risks. (2) Decisions can usually be reversed without damage to the image of the leader. (3) Nobody is maintaining a decision ''track record'' on Carlos. (4) Making no decision can be the worst decision of all.

Case Study 5: Robin does not appear to be ''ready'' to make a commitment to leadership preparation. It could be suggested to her that another year of management preparation (taking courses at night) could help her build a better base upon which she could launch her leadership talents at a later date. Robin will not be free to lead until her management skills reach a higher level.

NOTES

FOR OTHER FIFTY-MINUTE SELF-STUDY BOOKS
SEE ORDER FORM AT THE BACK OF THE BOOK.

NOTES

NOTES

FOR OTHER FIFTY-MINUTE SELF-STUDY BOOKS
SEE ORDER FORM AT THE BACK OF THE BOOK.

NOTES

FOR OTHER FIFTY-MINUTE SELF-STUDY BOOKS
SEE ORDER FORM AT THE BACK OF THE BOOK.

THE FIFTY-MINUTE SERIES

Quantity	Title	Code #	Price	Amount
	MANAGEMENT TRAINING			
	Self-Managing Teams	000-0	$7.95	
	Delegating For Results	008-6	$7.95	
	Successful Negotiation—Revised	09-2	$7.95	
	Increasing Employee Productivity	010-8	$7.95	
	Personal Performance Contracts—Revised	12-2	$7.95	
	Team Building—Revised	16-5	$7.95	
	Effective Meeting Skills	33-5	$7.95	
	An Honest Day's Work: Motivating Employees To Excel	39-4	$7.95	
	Managing Disagreement Constructively	41-6	$7.95	
	Training Managers To Train	43-2	$7.95	
	Learning To Lead	043-4	$7.95	
	The Fifty-Minute Supervisor—Revised	58-0	$7.95	
	Leadership Skills For Women	62-9	$7.95	
	Systematic Problem Solving & Decision Making	63-7	$7.95	
	Coaching & Counseling	68-8	$7.95	
	Ethics In Business	69-6	$7.95	
	Understanding Organizational Change	71-8	$7.95	
	Project Management	75-0	$7.95	
	Risk Taking	76-9	$7.95	
	Managing Organizational Change	80-7	$7.95	
	Working Together In A Multi-Cultural Organization	85-8	$7.95	
	Selecting And Working With Consultants	87-4	$7.95	
	PERSONNEL MANAGEMENT			
	Your First Thirty Days: A Professional Image in a New Job	003-5	$7.95	
	Office Management: A Guide To Productivity	005-1	$7.95	
	Men and Women: Partners at Work	009-4	$7.95	
	Effective Performance Appraisals—Revised	11-4	$7.95	
	Quality Interviewing—Revised	13-0	$7.95	
	Personal Counseling	14-9	$7.95	
	Attacking Absenteeism	042-6	$7.95	
	New Employee Orientation	46-7	$7.95	
	Professional Excellence For Secretaries	52-1	$7.95	
	Guide To Affirmative Action	54-8	$7.95	
	Writing A Human Resources Manual	70-X	$7.95	
	Winning at Human Relations	86-6	$7.95	
	WELLNESS			
	Mental Fitness	15-7	$7.95	
	Wellness in the Workplace	020-5	$7.95	
	Personal Wellness	021-3	$7.95	

THE FIFTY-MINUTE SERIES (Continued)

Quantity	Title	Code #	Price	Amount
	WELLNESS (CONTINUED)			
	Preventing Job Burnout	23-8	$7.95	
	Job Performance and Chemical Dependency	27-0	$7.95	
	Overcoming Anxiety	029-9	$7.95	
	Productivity at the Workstation	041-8	$7.95	
	COMMUNICATIONS			
	Technical Writing In The Corporate World	004-3	$7.95	
	Giving and Receiving Criticism	023-X	$7.95	
	Effective Presentation Skills	24-6	$7.95	
	Better Business Writing—Revised	25-4	$7.95	
	Business Etiquette And Professionalism	032-9	$7.95	
	The Business Of Listening	34-3	$7.95	
	Writing Fitness	35-1	$7.95	
	The Art Of Communicating	45-9	$7.95	
	Technical Presentation Skills	55-6	$7.95	
	Making Humor Work	61-0	$7.95	
	Visual Aids In Business	77-7	$7.95	
	Speed-Reading In Business	78-5	$7.95	
	Publicity Power	82-3	$7.95	
	Influencing Others	84-X	$7.95	
	SELF-MANAGEMENT			
	Attitude: Your Most Priceless Possession-Revised	011-6	$7.95	
	Personal Time Management	22-X	$7.95	
	Successful Self-Management	26-2	$7.95	
	Balancing Home And Career—Revised	035-3	$7.95	
	Developing Positive Assertiveness	38-6	$7.95	
	The Telephone And Time Management	53-X	$7.95	
	Memory Skills In Business	56-4	$7.95	
	Developing Self-Esteem	66-1	$7.95	
	Creativity In Business	67-X	$7.95	
	Managing Personal Change	74-2	$7.95	
	Stop Procrastinating: Get To Work!	88-2	$7.95	
	CUSTOMER SERVICE/SALES TRAINING			
	Sales Training Basics—Revised	02-5	$7.95	
	Restaurant Server's Guide—Revised	08-4	$7.95	
	Telephone Courtesy And Customer Service	18-1	$7.95	
	Effective Sales Management	031-0	$7.95	
	Professional Selling	42-4	$7.95	
	Customer Satisfaction	57-2	$7.95	
	Telemarketing Basics	60-2	$7.95	
	Calming Upset Customers	65-3	$7.95	
	Quality At Work	72-6	$7.95	
	Managing Quality Customer Service	83-1	$7.95	
	Quality Customer Service—Revised	95-5	$7.95	
	SMALL BUSINESS AND FINANCIAL PLANNING			
	Understanding Financial Statements	022-1	$7.95	
	Marketing Your Consulting Or Professional Services	40-8	$7.95	

THE FIFTY-MINUTE SERIES (Continued)

Quantity	Title	Code #	Price	Amount
	SMALL BUSINESS AND FINANCIAL PLANNING (CONTINUED)			
	Starting Your New Business	44-0	$7.95	
	Personal Financial Fitness—Revised	89-0	$7.95	
	Financial Planning With Employee Benefits	90-4	$7.95	
	BASIC LEARNING SKILLS			
	Returning To Learning: Getting Your G.E.D.	002-7	$7.95	
	Study Skills Strategies—Revised	05-X	$7.95	
	The College Experience	007-8	$7.95	
	Basic Business Math	024-8	$7.95	
	Becoming An Effective Tutor	028-0	$7.95	
	CAREER PLANNING			
	Career Discovery	07-6	$7.95	
	Effective Networking	030-2	$7.95	
	Preparing for Your Interview	033-7	$7.95	
	Plan B: Protecting Your Career	48-3	$7.95	
	I Got the Job!	59-9	$7.95	
	RETIREMENT			
	Personal Financial Fitness—Revised	89-0	$7.95	
	Financial Planning With Employee Benefits	90-4	$7.95	

OTHER CRISP INC. BOOKS

Quantity	Title	Code #	Price	Amount
	Desktop Publishing	001-9	$7.95	
	Stepping Up To Supervisor	11-8	$13.95	
	The Unfinished Business Of Living: Helping Aging Parents	19-X	$12.95	
	Managing Performance	23-7	$19.95	
	Be True To Your Future: A Guide To Life Planning	47-5	$13.95	
	Up Your Productivity	49-1	$10.95	
	Comfort Zones: Planning Your Future 2/e	73-4	$13.95	
	Copyediting 2/e	94-7	$18.95	
	Recharge Your Career	027-2	$12.95	
	Practical Time Management	275-4	$13.95	

VIDEO TITLE*

Quantity	Video Title*	Code #	Preview	Purchase	Amount
	Attitude: Your Most Priceless Possession	012-4	$25.00	$395.00	
	Quality Customer Service	013-2	$25.00	$395.00	
	Team Building	014-2	$25.00	$395.00	
	Job Performance & Chemical Dependency	015-9	$25.00	$395.00	
	Better Business Writing	016-7	$25.00	$395.00	
	Comfort Zones	025-6	$25.00	$395.00	
	Creativity in Business	036-1	$25.00	$395.00	
	Motivating at Work	037-X	$25.00	$395.00	
	Calming Upset Customers	040-X	$25.00	$395.00	
	Balancing Home and Career	048-5	$25.00	$395.00	
	Stress and Mental Fitness	049-3	$25.00	$395.00	

(*Note: All tapes are VHS format. Video package includes five books and a Leader's Guide.)

THE FIFTY-MINUTE SERIES
(Continued)

	Amount
Total Books	
Less Discount (5 or more different books 20% sampler)	
Total Videos	
Less Discount (purchase of 3 or more videos earn 20%)	
Shipping ($3.50 per video, $.50 per book)	
California Tax (California residents add 7%)	
TOTAL	

☐ Send volume discount information.

☐ Please send me a catalog.

☐ Mastercard ☐ VISA ☐ AMEX

Exp. Date _____

Account No. _____ Name (as appears on card) _____

Ship to: _____ Bill to: _____

_____ _____

_____ _____

_____ _____

Phone number: _____ P.O. # _____

All orders except those with a P.O.# must be prepaid.
For more information Call (415) 949-4888 or FAX (415) 949-1610.